MODERN**METAL**
GUITAR**TECHNIQUE**

Craft Powerful, Heavy Metal Guitar Riffs & Melodic Lines With Trivium's Matt Heafy

MATT**HEAFY**

FUNDAMENTAL**CHANGES**

Modern Metal Guitar Technique

Craft Powerful, Heavy Metal Guitar Riffs & Melodic Lines With Trivium's Matt Heafy

ISBN: 978-1-78933-460-9

Published by **www.fundamental-changes.com**

Copyright © 2025 Matthew Kiichi Heafy

Edited by Tim Pettingale

www.fundamental-changes.com

Join our free Facebook Community of Cool Musicians

www.facebook.com/groups/fundamentalguitar

Instagram: **FundamentalChanges**

For over 350 Free Guitar Lessons with Videos Check Out

www.fundamental-changes.com

Cover Image Copyright: Author photo used by permission

Contents

Introduction

Welcome to *Modern Metal Guitar Technique*, my first book with the awesome Fundamental Changes, which takes a deep dive into my playing style.

As a band, Trivium's guitar style has evolved over the course of many years and successive albums. We've moved from using standard tuned 6-string guitars to Drop D tuning, then Drop D with the whole guitar detuned a half step, then 7-string, and finally 7-string detuned a half step. In this book, we'll go on a similar journey: exploring drills, riffs and melodic ideas, and also breaking down sections of songs, that use these tunings.

I trust that the book in your hands will provide not only a comprehensive breakdown of my playing style, but give some insight into the progressive techniques you'll find in the genres of Thrash Metal, Metalcore, and Melodic Death Metal.

In the early days of Trivium, I was the sole guitar player and developed a style (out of necessity) that blended rhythm and lead techniques to fill the sonic space in the band's sound. That approach has remained with me, so here you'll find a blurring of the lines between what might be considered a rhythm part and a riff, or a riff and a lead line. To me, it's all about finding the right part for the song – one that will drive it forward and keep things engaging for the listener.

There is lots to learn here, and plenty of drills to push your playing limits as well as melodic examples. My hope is that you'll take the information here and use it to become a versatile modern Metal guitar player, increasing your technical proficiency, and taking inspiration from the musical examples to discover and establish your own unique voice.

Enjoy the ride!

Matthew Kiichi Heafy

Get the Audio

The audio files for this book are available to download for free from **www.fundamental-changes.com**. The link is in the top right-hand corner. Click "Download Audio" and choose your instrument. Select the title of this book from the menu, and complete the form to get your audio.

We recommend that you download the files directly to your computer (not to your tablet or phone) and extract them there before adding them to your media library. If you encounter any difficulty, we provide technical support within 24 hours via the contact form.

For over 350 free guitar lessons with videos check out:

www.fundamental-changes.com

Join our free Facebook Community of Cool Musicians

www.facebook.com/groups/fundamentalguitar

Tag us for a share on Instagram: **FundamentalChanges**

Chapter One – Warm-Up Drills & Foundational Rhythm Techniques

The Preparation Before Practice

Countless guitar players have asked me, "What should I practice?" Very few have ever asked, "*How* should I practice?" Yet, the act of *preparing* to practice is crucially important, and for that reason I'd like to pass along some advice on how to get ready to practice.

Whether I'm going to be practicing, recording or writing, I like to have everything set up before I begin. In other words, I prepare everything I'll need before starting to play, so that when I pick up the guitar, I can focus 100% on what I'm doing with no distractions.

In the world of cooking there is a concept known as *mise en place* – a French phrase that means "to gather" and "put everything in its place". Similarly, with guitar playing, by putting in place everything you need before you begin, you remove all barriers to effective practice.

So, what might this process involve? If you've seen my home "dojo", which I use for streaming and recording, you've probably noticed that I have everything set up, ready to go at all times. I don't like to waste time unplugging/re-plugging things before I can get started.

Whether you're a serious guitar player or an enthusiastic hobbyist who wants to take things more seriously, having a well-conceived setup with everything in place, working just as it should, is a vital precursor to serious practice.

Practically, this means having your amp and any effects you intend to use connected correctly and ready to go. It may also mean having headphones ready, set to the right level, if making a noise will upset your neighbors. Make sure your guitar is tuned up and new strings have been sufficiently played in. Get any materials you're going to use for practice (such as a book like this) ready on your music stand. Now, deal with any messages on your phone and set it to silent, or better still leave it another room. Finally, take a look at the time and decide how long you can spend in focused practice.

Ergonomics

As well as having a setup that's ready to go at a moment's notice, our posture plays a big role in how effectively we practice. I recommend being seated as the best way – ideally on a drum throne, or at the very least seated at the front of a chair without arms.

I also recommend using a classical guitarist's footstool. Look at a picture of how a classical player holds their guitar and you'll see that the instrument is tilted to an angle of about 30°. This is a great position for practice because it's very ergonomic. It greatly reduces the amount of tension placed upon the wrist of the fretting hand, especially when playing wide bends. It also allows for much easier access to the upper range of the guitar without stressing the wrist. Any time I'm practicing, and whenever I'm recording in the studio, this is most often how I'll be playing.

That said, it's good to practice playing standing up some of the time, so that you have a good, relaxed posture when you *have* to stand to play, such as during a live performance. For this, I recommend using a dual guitar strap. This special type of strap spreads the weight of the guitar over both shoulders. It doesn't distribute it 50/50 – more like 60/40 – but it does mean that the weight of the instrument is no longer borne by just one shoulder, and this certainly helps to prevent back/shoulder pain.

Another reason why it's good to practice while standing is that if you practice sitting the whole time, when you suddenly play standing up, you may find that your muscle memory doesn't respond in the way you expect. If you do a *lot* of live playing, you'll certainly want to practice while standing roughly 50% of the time.

Stretching

Most days when I'm at home I'm doing something physical. I often do an hour of Yoga practice each day, an hour of stretching, and I practice Brazilian Jujitsu 3-4 times per week. When I'm touring, it's not always possible to dedicate that amount of time, but on a show day I'll make sure I do a streamlined Yoga routine and some good stretching. I might also do some weights and Jujitsu, but I'm careful not to wear myself out, so that I save some energy for the actual performance.

Before practicing, I like to stretch my fingers by extending one arm, holding my hand upward (like I'm telling someone to stop) and pulling back on the fingers with the other hand. Then I'll rotate my arm so that the fingers are pointing toward the floor and repeat the stretch. I do both stretches on both hands and hold them for about ten seconds each. Make sure you stretch gently to begin with, and increase the stretch slowly. Next, repeat the same movements but focus on stretching the wrists rather than the fingers.

I also do biceps stretches by holding my arms out to the side, parallel to the floor in a T-shape, then tilting my wrists to point my fingers at the floor. You'll feel this pulling on the biceps. Next, you can do triceps, shoulders, neck, back and hamstring stretches – the works! I won't describe all these in detail, as there are plenty of demonstrations on YouTube, but the point is to stretch your body as much as possible to get rid of all tension and put yourself into as relaxed a posture as possible.

This might sound excessive to some, but I have always found that I play *much* better after I've exercised or stretched my body in this way and I highly recommend it.

The Benefits of a Structured Practice Approach

I can't stress enough the need for a structured approach to your practice. If you want to get better at what you do, aimless practice sessions full of noodling won't bring the results you want.

When you've dealt with your setup so that's it's always ready to go, you've stretched so that you're limber for playing, and you've gotten comfortable and prepared your posture… now what?

Here are my tips for effective practice:

1. Whatever you practice, *always* play to a metronome. Our internal sense of time is often quite different to reality, and the only way to improve it is by playing to a metronome to develop our timekeeping discipline.

2. Have a clear plan for what you're going to practice. You might, for example, take an exercise that is too intense for you when played at full tempo and slow it down, setting the metronome to a more modest pace that's achievable, then drill it for a while at that manageable pace. Over time, you can notch up the metronome 5bpm at a time until you can play the drill cleanly at full tempo. That's a practice plan that has a defined goal and a clear, desired outcome.

3. Make the time you have count. Highly focused practice that prioritizes quality over quantity will always yield better results. Even if you can only spare 20 minutes per day, a high quality 20 minutes daily will bring greater benefit than practicing for 1-2 hours once per week in an unfocussed manner without clear goals. And don't screw around on your phone or try and do something else at the same time!

With these principles in mind, let's move on to some of my recommended warm-up routines. Warming up is an often-neglected area of practicing the guitar, but I would suggest that it's a vital element, especially if you want to master some of the challenging techniques of modern Metal.

Warm-Up & Essential Drills

I like to begin my warm-ups by getting my finger coordination working effectively. I'll typically start with this exercise that I learned from John Petrucci. Here, we're using one finger per string to play adjacent strings using alternate down-up picking. The picking direction and fingering are indicated on the notation/TAB below. Here is the basic pattern:

Example 1a

We can take this pattern and move it across string sets like this:

Example 1b

Then we can play it ascending and descending to form a three-bar looping pattern.

Example 1c

We've played this at the modest tempo of 80bpm, which you'll probably find quite achievable. But as soon as we increase the tempo the drill becomes much more demanding, as it tests both our fretting hand dexterity and our alternate picking accuracy. One of the hardest things to do on guitar is to pick patterns that have only one note per string, so this is a good test.

Use this drill to lock in your hand coordination and, working with a metronome, up the tempo in 5bpm increments. A good challenge is to work your way towards being able to play it cleanly at 120bpm. Use a clean guitar sound for this exercise so that you can really hear how cleanly/accurately you're playing – don't disguise it with overdrive.

Once you're comfortable with the drill, you can change it up. Here we stay in fifth position, but this time start with the pinkie finger to reverse the drill. Work with this idea until you can play it cleanly at a reasonably quick tempo. Remember that accuracy is more important than speed because you're building muscle memory. If you speed up before you're ready, you'll just be training yourself to play badly faster!

Example 1d

We can turn this into a triplet exercise. This drill ascends three notes of the pattern, then doubles back to play three notes beginning on the second note of the pattern, and continues with this sequence. Because we're breaking up the four-note pattern, the whole sequence now takes nine bars to loop around.

Example 1e

Work with the previous pattern at various tempi. 90bpm is a good place to start once you've memorized the pattern, and you can gradually work your way up to 130bpm and beyond.

The next step in the warm-up is to move to two notes per string, and to involve different pairs of fingers in the exercise. For example, here is a simple pattern moving in half steps, using just the first and second fingers of the fretting hand.

Example 1f

We can take that pattern and develop it, moving to using the first and third fingers, then the first and fourth fingers (allocating one finger to each fret in position).

Example 1g

To increase the difficulty of this exercise, we can work with other finger combinations while omitting the first finger.

Here, we begin with half step intervals again, this time played with the second and third fingers. In bar four we start to work the second and fourth fingers playing whole step intervals. Finally, from bar seven we're using the third and fourth fingers to play half steps.

Playing patterns without the first finger will feel alien to you at first. To play with, say, just the third and fourth fingers demands much more concentration to keep up the accuracy and consistency.

Because your fretting hand is not used to using your fingers in this way, be aware of any tension creeping in. If you feel any discomfort at all, stop and take a break. However, if you can make this a part of your regular warm-up regimen, you'll strengthen your fretting hand and soon begin to see clear improvements in your picking coordination.

Example 1h

The next logical step is to practice some three-note-per-string patterns using different intervals. I like to use 1 2 4, 1 2 3, 1 3 4, and 2 3 4 patterns, and I normally change the rhythm to 1/8th note triplets.

Try this 1 2 4 pattern that ascends from the 5th fret, then moves up a half step on the top string before descending. Use strict alternate down-up picking as before.

Example 1i

We can extend this into a longer exercise moving through the four fingering permutations mentioned above. Fingerings are indicated in the notation/TAB only when they change to a new permutation.

Example 1j

Here's a 1 3 4 pattern with a bigger stretch, using whole step intervals, which also doubles back on itself.

Example 1k

Next, a doubling-back chromatic 1 2 3 4 exercise, which is my take on the Berklee exercise that has always been popular. We ascend three strings at a time, then jump back a string. On the top string, we shift up a half step, then reverse the pattern on the way down.

Example 11

We've looked at a range of warm-up exercises to get the fingers of the fretting hand working smoothly in coordination. Bear in mind that you can adapt these exercises to create new drills and challenge yourself further. For example, if a drill is ascending, reverse it and play it descending too.

Next, we're going to focus on the picking hand and work through some routines that are specifically aimed at sharpening up two main aspects of modern Metal technique.

Unlike the warm-ups, these drills are melodic exercises in themselves, and they act like a bridge into the core rhythm guitar ideas that are to come.

Building Downpicking Control and Stamina

Rapid and consistent downpicking with technical precision is an important feature of modern Metal, and I'm asked all the time, "How do I build my downpicking stamina?"

The answer is the metronome, coupled with the discipline to patiently build the technique over time. Just like developing muscle in the gym, it requires the consistent repetition of the right kind of drills.

Start with a simple power chord exercise like the one below. You can use a distorted sound here (because that's what you'll ultimately want to perform with, so you'll need to learn how to control it), and use palm muting throughout.

One tip for locking in with the metronome is to heavily accent the first beat of every bar. You may not want to do this all the time when you're playing a song, but it's helpful to begin with, as part of a warm-up exercise to lock in your timing.

Example 1m starts at the modest tempo of 90bpm, playing the power chord in 1/16th notes, but you'll quickly want to escalate that. Strive for accuracy and, over time, get the tempo into the 140bpm zone. However, don't rush to get there – take your time and aim for precision.

Example 1m

To make things more interesting, we can practice rapid downpicking with added accent notes on an adjacent string to create a pedal tone effect. Try this idea played in 1/8th note triplets. Make each of the accent notes on the fifth string pop out by picking them slightly harder. Start out at 90bpm but slowly notch up the tempo.

Example 1n

Let's extend this idea and give the fretting hand a little more work to do. Hold down the higher notes on the bottom string with the second finger. Try this at 120bpm and really lock in with the metronome's click.

Example 1o

Experiment with your own variations on this idea, adding your own accent notes to create a riff.

It's also a good idea to practice downpicking on a single string. This drill also includes accent notes. Use a heavier attack on the accents and add some fast, wide vibrato to the 1/8th note at the end of each bar. This breaks up the rhythm and prevents it from being boring, continuous chugging.

Example 1p

To practice downpicking with a larger chord shape, I like to use this 7 8 9 10 pattern that falls easily under the fingers. Your first finger will hold down the 7th fret of the A string, and the remaining fingers will fall in line on the adjacent strings.

Example 1q

You can move this shape around to make it more riff-like while building your downpicking stamina, using the bottom string as a pedal tone to bounce off.

Example 1r

You can also change up the pattern to 7 9 8 10 for variation.

Example 1s

And you can switch between the two shapes to give the fretting hand fingers more to think about!

Example 1t

Next, we can flip the original pattern upside down, so that the first finger is holding the 7th fret of the B string, and the pinkie is on the 10th fret of the A string.

We'll also change things up by moving the pattern through four frets instead of three.

Example 1u

Like the previous pattern, we can change the fingering on the middle strings for variation. This drill isn't the prettiest thing in the world, but it provides some contrast to the relentless downpicking of simple power chords.

Example 1v

Now let's look at a downpicking drill that is more like a riff, based around a simple four-note motif. Here is the core idea:

Example 1w

We can turn that into a downpicked riff using a low pedal tone. Note that we're also playing the rhythm as 1/8th note triplets now.

We can keep developing this idea by changing the bass note while keeping the motif going and, eventually, by changing the motif itself.

Example 1x

Alternate Picking Control

Next, we move on to alternate picking. There are two main styles of alternate picking in Metal: palm muted and what I call "lifted".

Palm-muted alternate picking is what you'd normally expect to hear in Thrash, and is a little more traditional for non-extreme Metal. Here's a riff-exercise that uses this technique.

Rest the palm of your picking hand lightly on the strings near the bridge and use down-up alternate picking to play the riff. If you were playing on a single string, you'd use strict down-up picking throughout. But when including accent chords, as here, the accent and the bass note that follows it are both downpicked, so that the picking hand effectively "bounces" between the low E and A strings. This approach gives us the attack and dynamics we're looking for.

It's a 1/16th note pattern organized into six-note groupings, so start with a moderate tempo and work your way up to around 125bpm.

Example 1y

I prefer to play alternate picked riffs without palm-muting, with the hand lifted away slightly from the strings, as I like the greater dynamic range that can be achieved this way.

To use this technique and stop it from becoming uncontrolled noise, it's important to have an anchor point for the fretting hand.

I wrap my pinkie finger underneath the high E string to provide an anchor point, and this keeps my hand in position, enabling me to alternate pick accurately and consistently. This technique is good for Black or Death Metal, as well as Melodic Death Metal, and I find it a lot more interesting than muted chugging.

Play through the following practice etude. First, find a way of anchoring your fretting hand that feels comfortable to you, and allows you to keep it close to the strings without muting them. Keep a loose wrist in the fretting hand and use strict down-up alternate picking.

You should notice right away that having a "lifted" fretting hand actually helps with keeping the wrist loose – as opposed to palm-muting, where the wrist can't move as freely.

The etude starts off simply, with notes played on individual strings, then alternates between the low E string and dyads on the A and D strings, so watch out for those!

Example 1z

It's time for a reminder that you should practice every example here to a metronome and focus on locking in with the click. It's easy to get sloppy with driving rhythms like these, and we want to ensure we're playing the same number of notes per bar and consistently in time. Nothing will improve your time more than the merciless metronome!

The following drill will help you to develop the discipline of picking single strings while also smoothly changing position.

Example 1z1

Here's another cool pattern for alternate picking that is more of a melodic riff than an exercise. You can also loop this idea around to turn it into a stamina building drill.

Example 1z2

Finally, a longer etude that combines alternate picking with moving chord accents, some of which have moving inner lines. Your picking hand will move back and forth over the low E and A strings to flip between the open bass note and the chord patterns.

Example 1z3

We've looked at some essential warm-up routines and also practiced the core picking techniques of modern Metal. In the next chapter, we'll build on what we've practiced and learn how to turn these techniques into useable riffs that we could employ in songs to make our rhythm parts more interesting.

Chapter Two – Turning Techniques Into Melodic Riffs

The role of the rhythm guitar in modern Metal is fundamental to the sound of the music, and the rhythm parts we create are vitally important in setting the mood, feel and energy of each track. In the previous chapter we spent time drilling the two main picking techniques used in this type of music, and in this chapter we're going to look at how to use those techniques to create some exciting riffs.

As I mentioned in the Introduction, when Trivium made our first album, *Ember to Inferno*, we were a three-piece band and I was the sole guitar player and vocalist. In fact, we tried to find a second guitarist, but just didn't come across the right person at that time. So, it fell to me to cover both rhythm and lead guitar duties.

Born out of necessity, it made sense for me to try to create parts that contained elements of both rhythm and lead, and you'll see this approach in the ideas in this chapter.

I've always found that marriage of rhythm and melody really interesting, and you can incorporate this technique into your playing whether you're the only guitar player in your band, or if you're working with another guitarist.

Downpicked Riffs

First, let's look at three riffs that use straight downpicking technique.

These ideas are played in Drop-D tuning, but then the whole guitar is tuned down a further half step. This helps to create a powerful sound, incredibly rich in harmonics – especially when using the lowest string as a pedal tone to work against.

Consistent downpicking adds to the power and dynamics of this idea. Strive for picking accuracy as you bounce between the low pedal tone and the notes on the fifth and fourth strings. Good palm muting is essential here, especially when playing a string skip.

The low E string is now tuned down to C#, and this riff is built around the C# Phrygian Dominant scale, which contains the notes C#, D, F, F#, G#, A, B.

The Phrygian Dominant is the fifth mode of the Harmonic Minor scale and fits over a dominant 7 chord.

Because it has an augmented second interval between the second and third scale degrees, the scale conjures up an exotic, almost Middle Eastern vibe and is an interesting choice to play over a dominant chord.

In the Berklee College system, this scale also goes by the alternative name of Mixolydian b9 b13, and has been used in Jazz-Rock Fusion by players like Mike Stern. It also lends itself well to Gypsy Jazz!

Example 2a

Next up, play through this downpicked chord-riff in 6/8 time. The idea here is to keep a C# power chord (C# and G#) going and intersperse it with chord accents. Throughout bars 1-4, these are played as dyads (two-note chords) on the fifth and fourth strings.

In bar one we have a C#m dyad consisting of just the root note and the b3. In bar two, it's an E major, in bar three B major, and in bar four D#m.

In bars 5-8, these chords are moved onto the fifth and sixth strings and played as inversions. So, in bar five, we have a C#m inversion moving to a D#m inversion, and in bar six we have E major and B major inversions.

In the final two bars, we play a back-cycling, descending progression that aims to get us back to that C# power chord.

Listen to the audio example to nail down the timing and watch out for that 6/8 rhythm.

Example 2b

We've looked at a single-note riff and a mini-chord riff, so let's complete this section with a downpicking riff that uses bigger chord forms.

Note that this example is played in 12/8 time.

12/8 means that there are twelve 1/8th notes per bar. You can still count each bar as "1 2 3 4" but each count will be worth three 1/8th notes i.e., "**1**23, **2**23, **3**23, **4**23".

Once again, we're playing off a sixth string pedal tone. Interest is created in the rhythm by playing chord stabs on the first two 1/8th notes of the first group of three, and again on the last group of three in each bar.

This pattern repeats for the first six bars, but we deviate from it in bars 7-8, where the second set of stabs is played earlier, on the penultimate group of three in the bar.

Each chord form played here is an octave with one extra note added on top. For example, in bar one we have a C# octave plus an E note. The E is the minor 3rd, creating a C#m chord. In bar three, it's a C# octave plus an F# on top (the sus4), etc.

You'll need to position your fretting hand to mute the un-played open D string in this example, which you can do by lightly resting your first finger on it while fretting the notes on the A string.

Example 2c

Alternate Picked Riffs

Next, we'll look at two riffs that use alternate down-up picking.

The first is a fast-tempo riff that you might use to generate momentum in a song. With a focus on single notes, it's the type of idea that can cut through a band mix and grab the audience's attention. This 16-bar pattern could provide the main guitar part for a complete song.

This is a 12/8 time riff at a quick tempo, and the challenge for you here is to keep that low pedal tone going while arpeggiating the chords.

The harmony behind this idea comes from the C# Harmonic Minor scale (C#, D#, E, F#, G#, A, B#).

If we take that scale and harmonize it (i.e. take the first note of the scale and stack two notes a 3rd interval apart on top, then move to the second note and repeat the process, etc.) we get the resulting set of triads:

C# minor, D# diminished, E augmented, F# minor, G# major, A major and B# diminished.

We can extend these triads to become 7th chords by stacking three rather than two notes a 3rd apart on each scale tone, resulting in the following set of chords:

C#min(Maj7), D#m7b5, EMaj7#5, F#m7, G#7, AMaj7 and B#dim7.

Using this idea, the chord progression for this etude looks like this:

| C#m | % | F#m | % |

| D#m7b5 | % | C#m | % |

| G#7 | % | A major | % |

| G#7 | % | C#m | % |

Play through it now using strict down-up alternate picking.

Example 2d

```
    9                    10                    11                    12
T
A ---0-5-8----7----8-5-0-5-8----7----8-5--0-0-0-0-0-0-0-0-5-8----7----8-5--0-7-10----8----10-7-0-7-10----8----10-7--0-0-0-0-0-0-0-0-7-10----8----10-7
B
```

```
    13                    14                    15                    16
T
A ---0-4·7----5----7-4-0-4-7----5----7-4--0-0-0-0-0-0-0-0-4·7----5----7-4--0-5-8----7----8-5-0-5-8----7----8-5--0-5-8----7----8-5-0-5-8----7----8-5
B
```

Here's another single-note pedal tone etude, played at a high tempo and alternate picked. The first half of this riff uses the open fourth string as the pedal tone (a C# note with our lowered tuning), then switches onto the sixth string for the latter half (also C#).

Although C# is our pedal note, this time the melody notes come from the F# Harmonic Minor scale:

F#, G#, A, B, C#, D, E#

Focus on your picking accuracy here and work with a metronome to get your alternate picking timing sharp. This is a fast riff, so practice it slow to begin with, then gradually increase the tempo.

Example 2e

```
    1                                              2
   ∏ V ∏ V ∏ V ∏ V ∏ V ∏ V ∏ V ∏ V
T
A ---12-0—0-10-0—0-12-0—0-0—0-0—0-0—0--13—0-10—0-12-0—8—0-10—0-7—0-8—0-5—0
B
```

```
    3                                              4
T
A ---12-0—0-10-0—0-12-0—0-0—0-0—0-0—0--1—0—0—0-4—0—0—5—0—0-7—0—0—
B
```

5
6
T
A
B
12—0—0—10—0—0—12—0—0—0—0—0—0—0—0—0
17—0—13—0—16—0—12—0—13—0—10—0—12—0—8—0
7
8
12—0—0—10—0—0—12—0—0—0—0—0—0—0—0—0
5—0—0—0—7—0—0—0—8—0—0—0—4—0—0—0
9
10
12—0—0—10—0—0—12—0—0—0—0—0—0—0—0—0
13—0—10—0—12—0—8—0—10—0—7—0—8—0—5—0
11
12
12—0—0—10—0—0—12—0—0—0—0—0—0—0—0—0
1—0—0—0—4—0—0—0—5—0—0—0—7—0—0—0
13
14
12—0—0—10—0—0—12—0—0—0—0—0—0—0—0—0
17—0—13—0—16—0—12—0—13—0—10—0—12—0—8—0
15
16
12—0—0—10—0—0—12—0—0—0—0—0—0—0—0—0
5 5 5
7 7 7
8 8 8
7 7 7
4 4 4

Tremolo Picked Riffs

Next, we're going to explore four riffs played with a new technique we've not yet explored: *tremolo picking*.

On the face of it, this technique could be mistaken for alternate picking, because the picking hand is moving down and up throughout. So, what sets tremolo picking apart?

First, it's a continuous motion – there are no breaks in the picking action.

Second, it's a type of alternate picking performed at a very fast speed. It's often used to play just one note very fast, and you may have heard this done in mainstream rock, country or rockabilly music. But it is also used in modern Metal to play chords as well as single notes to create an intense wall of sound.

Lastly, compared to normal alternate picking, tremolo is harder to master because it places rigorous demands on the player, both in terms of picking accuracy and physical stamina.

While it's common in rock guitar technique to play tremolo on a single string, we're making things significantly more difficult in the first riff below by quickly jumping to notes on adjacent strings.

Here is some guidance to help you master tremolo technique:

- Focus on keeping your picking arm and wrist relaxed. If you try to pick faster by flexing your arm muscles, your forearm and wrist will begin to tense up, and this is the opposite of what you're aiming for. The speed comes from a relaxed posture

- Program your muscle memory well by practicing the continuous down-up motion at slower speeds initially. Concentrate on sounding each note for the same duration, so that it sounds even. It's hard to resist the urge to rush and play too fast too soon, but hold back and program in that consistency. Then, when you do speed up, the accuracy will be there

- Practice with a metronome set to a modest tempo and play 1/4 notes to begin with – one note per click. When you're accurate with the 1/4th notes, double it up to 1/8th notes but play to the same 1/4 note click. Work on ironing out any inaccuracies in your technique at this new level, until you can play 1/8th notes consistently in time. Next, go for playing 1/16th notes, but double up the metronome click to play an 1/8th note pulse. Repeat this process at different tempi. If you find yourself playing sloppily at any tempo, pull it back and practice slightly slower until you can't get it wrong, then sneak the tempo back up

In the audio example, I'm playing at circa 180bpm, so your challenge is to start slow and gradually work your way up to match my tempo.

Example 2f

Although tremolo is often played on single notes, I like to tremolo pick mini-chords and create riffs by moving notes around the shapes, as in the tremolo picked rhythm part below.

For this example, imagine you're playing a three-note-per-string pattern with your fretting hand, spanning frets 3-7.

For bars 1-2, place your first finger on the sixth string at the 3rd fret and keep it anchored there, even though you won't actually pick that note. Place your second finger on the fifth string, 5th fret, and keep that finger anchored there too. Now place your third finger on the 5th fret of the fourth string.

With all three fingers in place, play the riff in bars 1-2 by using your fourth finger to play the notes at the 7th fret of the fourth string. Play the notes at the 5th fret of that string with the third finger, lifting it up to sound the notes at the 3rd fret.

Your hand position will change for bars 3-4. Now, you'll anchor your first finger at the 2nd fret of the sixth string for stability, and your third finger will be anchored at the 4th fret of the fifth string and won't move. This time the fourth and second fingers will do the work of sounding the moving notes.

Using this anchoring principle, work out what fingerings you should use to play the riffs in the higher register in the most ergonomic and efficient way.

The rhythm part uses the C# Harmonic Minor scale (C#, D#, E, F#, G#, A, B#) throughout.

Example 2g

The next rhythm part strums full four-note chords. The harmony of this idea moves between chords taken from the E Harmonic Minor and C# Harmonic Minor scales – an interval of a minor 3rd apart – resulting in a dark, ethereal sounding progression.

Here, I've played with the quality of the D#m7♭5 chord that occurs naturally in C# Harmonic Minor, so that we have a straight D#m sound, but also a D#7sus to D#7 movement in the final two bars.

The big challenge with this rhythm part is tremolo strumming across all the middle strings, excluding the sixth and first string. Also remember, this is played with a "lifted" hand position. As a result, it demands a high level of picking hand accuracy with your strumming, so that you don't catch any strings that shouldn't be played.

On the audio, I'm playing this in 1/16th notes at circa 170bpm, so it also places some big demands on your strumming consistency and timing. Work to ensure the strums sound even – both in their note length and volume.

Example 2h

Next up is a hard driving riff. It's the type of idea you could use to inject any rhythm part with energy and momentum, while still leaving some sonic space for the other band instruments to occupy – in contrast to the fat, full sound of the previous example.

The rhythm is unusual here as we have three bars in 3/4 time signature, followed by a bar of 5/4 as a turnaround. I played the sequence twice on the audio example, but you should loop it around several times before going to the final bar of 4/4 to finish.

Example 2i

Here is an example of how you can take an idea like Example 2i (now converted into 4/4 time signature) and combine the rhythm part with a lead guitar melody to create a riff that sounds like two complementary guitar parts, fused together.

What makes this idea work is alternating the bars between rhythm and melody, so that the lead guitar element never feels too isolated from the driving rhythm.

The rhythm is tricky to master here because we begin each odd numbered bar with a longer 1/4 note before jumping into the 1/16th note rhythm. Play through it slowly with a metronome to nail down both parts.

Example 2j

As a contrast to a driving rhythm part, perhaps in a breakdown section of a tune, you can use an embellishment technique such as hammer-ons to create an interesting instrumental section.

Here we're using a C# note as the pedal tone on both the open sixth and fourth strings, and over the 4/4 pulse we're playing 1/8th note triplets. The first note of each triplet is played with a downstroke, then the subsequent two notes are hammered on.

This means you'll play a "hammer-on from nowhere" with your first finger i.e., hammering onto the 5th fret, having picked the open string. Then you'll play a hammer-on from the 5th to 8th fret with your fourth finger, due to the stretch.

Be mindful of any tension creeping into the fretting hand when playing an idea like this, as hammering on with the pinkie finger quickly becomes fatiguing.

Example 2k

Here's one final example that combines rhythm and lead parts, also using hammer-ons to embellish the melody. We've switched to 3/4 time for this example. Like Example 2j, I've chosen to integrate the parts by alternating between rhythm and melody, so that the listener never feels disconnected from either idea.

Notice that there is only one chord in this idea during bar one, so mostly the "rhythm part" here is played with single notes. The riff still works well because it functions like a question and answer phrase: the bass notes make a musical statement which is answered by the melody, and this alternates all the way through. We don't always have to play full chords to convey an effective rhythm part.

Example 2l

```
5                                              6  ┌─3─┐              ┌─3─┐
P.M.------┐      P.M.------┐

T
A  3      3-3-3-3-3   7   3-3-3-3-3        3─5─3───3     7─4─4─5─4      4
B                                                7           7         7─7─5

7                          8  ┌─3─┐                    9
P.M.------┐   P.M.-----┐

T
A  2   2-2-2-2-2   3  2-2-2-2-3      2─3─2───2   5─4─3─1     1       0
B                                         5         5─5─2   5─2     0
```

To close out this chapter, we'll look at a practical example of how the principles we've learned can be applied in the context of a song. We'll do this by breaking down some of the ideas used in the tune *Ember to Inferno* from the very first Trivium record of the same name, mentioned at the start of this chapter.

Because I was the sole guitar player at that time, I tried to come up with parts that combined elements of straight rhythm guitar and more lead guitar oriented riffs and melodic lines. This is a useful skill for any player to develop.

This song is played in standard tuning, but the whole guitar is lowered a half step, so that the low E string sounds as Eb on the audio.

We'll look at the part played throughout the verse first, breaking it into three parts.

The fast riff used for the first part is played using downpicking only. At full speed the tune is circa 240bpm during the fastest section, and this creates a challenge for the picking hand, which has to move very quickly. It's the right technique for this particular song, to bring it alive and give it the attack/dynamics the music demands.

After the initial power chords, the riff in Example 2m is played on the sixth and fifth strings, and since it's played all downpicked, the picking hand needs to accurately "bounce" between those two strings. Use some subtle palm muting with the picking hand to control the un-played strings, without actually anchoring your palm on the strings. In other words, allow your hand to just lightly touch the strings as part of the downpicking motion, without fully choking them.

An important part of the dynamics of this riff is created by the fretting hand. I like to play the notes on the fifth string by tapping my fingers onto the fretboard rather than pre-fretting the notes before they are played. So, having picked the open sixth string, I'll tap my first finger onto the 7th fret of the fifth string, rather than fretting it, then I'll tap my second finger onto the 9th fret, and so on.

This approach creates a more percussive, exciting part that sounds quite different from fretting and playing the notes. Notice that, as the riff ends ready to loop around, I apply some wide vibrato to the last note on the fifth string 10th fret.

The use of vibrato is important to me in general. Players use it all the time in lead soloing, but it can be extremely effective in composing a distinctive rhythm part. Here, it creates movement and allows the part to breathe in a way that wouldn't be possible if it were just played straight.

The note choices come from the E Melodic Minor scale, which contains the notes E, F#, G, A, B, C#, D#. The riff begins on the E root note then moves up the scale. On the record you'll hear a higher harmony part being played. This is the main riff harmonized into 3rds (so it begins on G, the third note of the scale). Remember that the recorded pitches will sound a half step lower!

Example 2m

The next two bars of the verse part switch to a more traditional rhythm part.

The idea here is to play four 1/16th notes on the sixth string then hit a chord. For this, you'll change to playing the notes on the sixth string using alternate down-up picking, then hit the chord with a downstroke.

The fretting hand is holding down a barre chord shape at the 8th fret for the chord-plus-melody bars. Place your first finger on the sixth string, 8th fret; third finger on the fifth string, 10th fret; and second finger on the fourth string, 9th fret. You can now use your fourth finger to play the moving notes.

The shifting notes on the fourth string create different variations of the underlying C chord: first Csus2, then CMaj7, and finally a straight C5 chord.

Example 2n

After these bars, we go back to the motif idea of Example 2m, but rather than using the open sixth string as a pedal tone, we modulate the riff. First, we move into 5th position and play the pedal tone note on the sixth string, 5th fret. Keep your third finger anchored on the fifth string, 7th fret, and play the moving notes with your fourth finger.

Next, move up to 9th position and repeat the process: the first finger will play the pedal tone note on the sixth string, 7th fret, with the third finger anchored at the 9th on the fifth string, and the fourth finger taking care of the notes that move around the shape.

You'll only hold this last shape briefly, however, because you'll need to quickly break out of it to play the last phrase of the riff as octaves. Playing the melody in a different way adds some interest and a different tonal dynamic.

In this section, the notes come from the E Natural Minor scale, so they sound more consonant or "inside" than the beginning E Melodic Minor line.

Example 2o

Let's now put those parts together and practice the full verse rhythm part. Notice in bar twelve that having played the octave at the 10th/12th frets, I move a half step below then slide back into position. It's a subtle movement, so on the notation the slide in from below is shown as grace notes (barely heard preceding notes).

Example 2p

On the song recording, everything we've played so far is repeated, then we move into the pre-chorus section. Here, we play some big, sustained power chords interspersed with lead guitar fills.

For the power chords, I like to hit the sixth string with a downstroke, catching the fifth string as well, push through, then hit the fifth string again on the way back up with an upstroke. This all happens very quickly, but it's an effective way of cleanly sounding the chord twice, and at the same time as controlling the string noise.

Each melodic fill is different and the second idea, played at the 10th fret, should be executed with fast tremolo picking rather than straight alternate picking. Then we alternate between octaves and chord voicings in a strumming pattern.

Example 2q

The opening four bars of the next section of the song show how a simple idea can blur the lines between rhythm and lead, as we move from chugging power chords to strummed octaves. It's the change in tonal texture here that makes the part work.

In bars 5-8, the last part of the previous example is repeated but we end the section in bar eight with more power chords.

Example 2r

47

Next up is a staccato chord section, where the chords are punched out with two hits, and space is left in between. The use of silence in riffs is greatly underrated! What we leave out can be just as effective as what we put it.

You'll begin this part with a wide, spread chord voicing. It uses the open sixth string, then you'll fret the 7th fret of the fifth string with your first finger, and the 12th fret of the fourth string with your fourth finger.

If this feels like a big stretch, you can minimize it by bringing your elbow more into your body, and rotating the wrist of your fretting hand so that your fretting hand moves away from the neck a little, and the open palm is exactly parallel to the fretboard. Usually, when we play regular stuff, the palm of the fretting hand is angled away from the neck slightly, so here we're bringing it into line. As soon as we do this, the stretch becomes manageable.

To ensure we get a "clean" silence between each chord hit after strumming the chords, lightly rest the fingers of your fretting hand across all the strings. This becomes especially important when you're playing really loud on stage and everything you play, good or bad, can be heard very clearly!

While keeping your first finger anchored on the 7th fret of the fifth string, the fourth finger moves from the 12th fret of the fourth string to play the 10th fret. Then the third finger takes over to play the note at the 9th.

I like to call the first chord voicing a "jazz chord". It's essentially an E7, but with no 3rd. Instead, we have the low E of the open string, the octave E at the 7th fret, then the b7 at the 12th.

When the fourth finger moves down a whole step to play the 10th fret, this turns the chord into an E augmented, made up of the E octave pattern plus a #5 interval on top.

When we play the note at the 9th fret, we turn the shape into an E power chord: an E octave plus the 5th.

Example 2s

Next, the rhythm part for the chorus. This idea is one of the most distinctive parts of the tune, flipping between low chords and a melodic phrase with heavy vibrato.

After hitting the low, three-note power chord, you'll play a slide into the 5th fret of the fourth string, then pick the 4th fret, adding wide vibrato. I tend to play the slide with my fourth finger, letting the third finger come behind it to drop onto the 4th fret for the vibrato note. I add a slight bit of vibrato on the pinkie finger note too.

It's not wrong if you prefer to play it using your third and second fingers if you feel your fourth finger lacks the strength for the slide and quick vibrato.

I play it the same way, leading with the pinkie when the motif is played higher, with notes on the 9th and 7th frets of the fourth string.

Notice here the chord shapes used for the C and D chords in between the vibrato motif. I could have played straight power chords here, with the root notes on the fifth string and the 5th interval on the fourth string. The choice to add in the 5th again, an octave below on the sixth string, gives it a nice twist and really thickens up the sound. The way the chord is voiced means that there is a 4th interval between the low G note and the C note on the adjacent string, creating a dense and much more powerful sound.

This part ends with a hammer-on/pull-off lick.

Example 2t

In Trivium's evolution, we began with standard tuned guitar, then moved to using Drop D tuning for the majority of tunes, before finally turning to a 7-string guitar approach. In the next chapter, I'll break down one of our most popular songs played in Drop D. Then, in the chapters that follow, we'll look at a series of tunes written for 7-string.

Chapter Three – Drop-D Rhythm Guitar

One of the tunes I get asked about a lot is *Suffocating Sight* from our second record, *Ascendancy*, so here I want to break down the ideas used in that tune and show how some of the rhythm techniques we've been learning translate into guitar parts in the context of this song.

For this piece the guitar is tuned to Drop D – so the low E string is tuned down a whole step to D, while the other strings remain untouched.

Throughout Trivium's history and evolution as a band, my main focus guitar-wise has been to be the best rhythm player I can possibly be, and to come up with interesting and challenging parts. I've been told that many an accomplished player has struggled to nail this tune and therefore I think it's a good piece for you to learn. It will help to refine your technique and also build your stamina. What's interesting about it is how it blends the techniques of downpicking and alternate picking.

We'll look at the different sections of the rhythm part, beginning with the intro, going into the verse, then the pre-chorus, and finally the chorus.

The song begins with a low power chord rhythm part. The chords are played with a 1/16th note rhythm, which is punctuated with 1/8th note rests to break it up. Bars one and two are divided up into the same rhythm: four 1/16th notes, an 1/8th note rest, six 1/16th notes, an 1/8th note rest, then two 1/16th notes. This broken pattern comes around again in bars five and six.

These are three-note power chords. We have the root note on the fifth string, the 5th of the chord on the fourth string, then the 5th added in again in the lower octave on the sixth string.

The first chord in bar one is a compact voicing of G minor. Visually, it looks a lot like the added 5th power chords we played at the end of the previous chapter, but now we're playing in Drop D, so the intervals have changed. Without the dropped bottom string, it would be a stretch to play this voicing. We have a G note on the bottom string (played at the 5th fret), a D on the fifth string 5th, fret, and a Bb on the fourth string 8th fret.

When we lower that Bb note a half step to A for the second chord in the sequence it gives us a Gsus2 chord. When we lower the moving note on the fourth string down a whole step to G, we end up with a G5 power chord that includes the root octave.

In bars 3-4 and 7-8, the rhythm is strummed with a down-up alternate motion. Here, instead of breaking up the rhythm with 1/8th note rests, the 1/16th notes are tied, so that any punctuation is much more subtle.

The notes on the fifth and fourth strings are the same ones we've played already, though in a different order, but we've replaced the G note at the 5th fret with the low open D.

This means we have adjacent D notes on the bottom two strings, while the notes on the fourth string move. When we play an A note on the fourth string 7th fret, that gives us a D5 power chord. When we move the A down a whole step to a G at the 5th fret, that gives us a Dsus. And when we move it up to a Bb note at the 8th fret, that gives us a D augmented or D#5.

Example 3a

Next, we're into the verse section of the song, which begins with a dramatic change of tempo. The introduction was played at 112bpm and now we immediately push it up to circa 180bpm. This is one of the things that has made this song challenging for others to play over the years.

Before we look at this idea, let me say a quick word about the rhythm used during this section. Perhaps because it is somewhat disguised by the speed of the tune, and because the low notes are grouped in threes, some have erroneously claimed that it's a triplet-based riff. Actually, it's played in straight 1/16th notes, but in each group of four, one 1/16th note is omitted.

If we count the rhythm in 1/16th notes i.e., "1-e-&-a, 2-e-&-a", I'm missing out the "a" from each group of four notes. Here's the rhythm, with the rest notes played with muted strings to begin with, so you can get a feel for what you need to play (these chords don't belong to the song and there's no audio for this example!)

Example 3b

Omitting the "a" beat every time does result in the notes being played in groups of three with an urgent, galloping rhythm, but they are still straight 1/16th notes. It can take a moment to get your head around this if you've never thought of doing it before, so practice it slowly to begin with to lock in the rhythm.

In the first couple of bars of the verse, this rhythmic pattern is applied to the melodic line below. The main challenge here is to become adept at switching seamlessly between the fast low notes and the phrase that fits around them. Loop this idea around to get comfortable with the switch.

Make a first finger barre at the 5th fret. Downpick the 1/16th note figure using palm muting. Then, play a hammer-on from the 5th to 6th fret on the A string using a downstroke. Next, pick the 8th fret of the D string with an upstroke, followed by the 6th fret of the A string with a downstroke to complete the phrase.

Example 3c

The next part of the verse riff features mixed 1/8th and 1/16th note rhythms. You'll begin playing in 5th position then, at the end of bar one, you'll need to shift position with slides to get into 9th position for the rest of the riff.

The picking hand technique I use to play the riff in bars 7-8 I call "down-down-down-up-down". We've looked at strictly downpicked rhythms, alternate picked rhythms and tremolo, but this idea produces a different rhythmic effect that I've used in several Trivium tunes. I sometimes call it the "John Wayne" rhythm and you'll understand why.

The pattern is two 1/8th notes played with downstrokes, followed by two 1/16th notes. The 1/16th notes are alternate picked, down-up, and this is followed by another 1/8th note, downpicked. It's the "interruption" of the 1/16th notes that gives this rhythm its galloping skip.

Although this sounds straightforward in theory, the tempo of this tune makes it challenging to play. I recommend learning the riff slowly, paying attention to the picking pattern to program the sequence into muscle memory. If you do a good job of programming the picking movements, you'll be able to speed up smoothly.

Example 3d

Now we'll combine these two parts to complete the pattern that is played throughout the verse.

Example 3e

For interest, this is the part that the second guitar plays to the verse pattern – at times dovetailing with the first guitar, and at other times doubling up on the riff. There's no audio for this example, but you can use it to play along with the first guitar part.

Example 3f

Next comes the pre-chorus section, which we'll look at in two parts. First there is an eight-bar section with a series of chord accents, each of which bounces off a different pedal tone note.

It's the moving bass notes at the center of this idea that create the tension which drives the part forward. The heart of it is the Dsus chord in bar one. Tension is created when the bass note drops a half step to Db, and the higher note moves up to an A. This new chord could be interpreted as a DMaj7, with the 7th in the bass.

Next, the bass note moves up a whole step to Eb, while the top note moves up a half step – an Eb5 power chord. In bar four, we play an F in the bass with an A on top – a straight root plus 3rd F major chord. To finish the pattern, the F moves up to F# while the A note remains in place. This gives us an F#m chord, with the A note now functioning as a minor 3rd rather than a major 3rd.

Example 3g

In the second half of the pre-chorus, the chords you've just played are repeated, played as sustained power chords on their own. The pre-chorus ends by playing a galloping rhythm on a single G note.

This rhythm is tricky to get right, not least due to the tempo. Visually, on the TAB you can see that it's a combination of two single notes (both 1/8th notes) and three groups of three notes (two 1/16ths followed by an 1/8th note).

To understand how the rhythm works, let's first of all notice that the single note at the beginning of bar nine obviously falls on beat one of the bar. Then, the two groups of three notes at the end of the bar begin on beats 3 and 4 respectively. Now we can just concern ourselves with fitting in the notes that come after beat 1 and before beat 3.

If we count the bar in 1/16th notes, 1-e-&-a, 2-e-&-a, etc., the first group of three notes begins on the "& of beat 1. The single note that follows falls on the "&" of beat 2.

Play the whole rhythm very slowly to a metronome and lock in the pattern.

Example 3h

Now we arrive at the chorus pattern for *Suffocating Sight*. There are two guitar parts happening on the recording. The first is a combined chords and melody part. The second guitar, which we'll look at it a moment, plays a higher melodic line to complement it.

To play this part, we're going to use two positions on the neck and hold those shapes while the melody notes move around them.

First, place your first finger at the 5th fret across the bottom three strings. For the melody, your pinkie finger will take care of the note at the 8th fret, fourth string. Your third finger will then play the 7th fret, and your first finger will already be holding down the 5th fret. Remove all your fingers to play the bottom three strings open.

You'll take a similar approach to play the first position chords and melody. With your first finger, hold down the bottom three strings at the 1st fret. To play the ascending melody, use your third finger to play the 3rd fret of the fourth string, and your pinkie to play the 5th fret.

You'll then need to slide up to play the final two chords in bar two. Add lots of wide, fast vibrato to the A note on the 7th fret at the end of the bar.

Example 3i

The higher guitar part that you'll hear on the record is shown here for reference. There is no audio for this example, but it's straightforward to play. Use the TAB to play along with the audio for the previous guitar part, or the album recording.

Example 3j

On the album recording, you'll hear that next comes a brief interlude, followed by some dramatic chord accents that lead into the guitar solo. Then the original riffs kicks in again, but now at a much faster tempo (circa 222bpm).

Now you have all the essential parts of the tune, so try them out by playing along with the album track.

Chapter Four – Seven-String Guitar Riffs

The history of the 7-string guitar goes back way further than most players realize. The instrument has been around more than 230 years, so it's not a modern invention. But the electric 7-string, with its ability to be amplified and have its sound further enhanced with effects, has been a game-changer and one that was quickly embraced by the Metal guitar community.

In recent years, Trivium has embraced the 7-string for our recordings and live performances. A standard 7-string guitar is like a standard six-string with an additional string. The extra string can be a high or a low one, but it's most common to have an added low B string, so that the guitar is tuned B E A D G B E.

In Trivium, we lower that a half step, so the tuning becomes Bb Eb Ab Db Gb Bb Eb.

Compared to the low E of a standard six-string, the low Bb of a detuned 7-string is a diminished 5th interval away – in other words, three whole steps (six frets). What's so interesting about this tuning is that we're extending the range of our instrument into bass territory, and this opens up completely new sonic possibilities due to the way the guitar resonates with the bass.

In this chapter we'll look at some ideas where that low string becomes an essential part of the riff or song at hand, rather than being an add-on. We'll start with a couple of cool example riffs (and I encourage you to write your own, similar ideas) then we'll look at some sections of Trivium tunes where the seventh string plays an essential role.

To begin, here's a simple pedal tone idea on one string. This could sound pretty routine on a regular six-string, but here we gain the benefit of both the additional low string, and the further half step detune to take it to Bb. I think you'll agree the resulting sound is pretty cool.

Example 4a

Riffs that utilize the open seventh string and combine it with a higher melody can sound huge compared to standard tuning as this hammer-on riffs demonstrates. This riff includes a string skip to add some separation between the low pedal tone and the melody notes. The effect is almost like a bass and a guitar playing counterpoint parts, and it fills a huge amount of sonic space.

Look out for the changes of rhythm in this lick. There are two bars of 3/4 followed by a bar of 5/4 that cycle around, and also a couple of bars of 4/4 to keep the riff shifting its axis. You can use this idea to sharpen up your picking hand with the string skips, and it's also a good workout to make sure your timing is on point.

Example 4b

Now let's look at the kind of ideas the detuned 7-string can facilitate in a songwriting setting. The riffs used in the Trivium tune *In the Court of the Dragon* are a natural progression from the previous two riff examples and highlight the potential of the low seventh string in a melodic context.

First, let's look at this four-bar repeating riff. It relies heavily on the seventh string to add a darkness and depth to the sound.

At the end of bar one, you'll hit the final note on the 8th fret and hold it over into the next bar, then play the 7th fret. Be sure to add some dramatic, wide vibrato to both these notes.

I often say that in this tune, we capture the genealogy of the Trivium sound, because it contains a nod to each era of our sound, and this particular riff really captures the sound of the *Ember to Inferno* record. It's also inspired by the Swedish Melodic Death Metal scene that came out of Gothenburg.

The line is played using all downpicking and the core idea, in bars one and three, is that it's ascending the Bb Natural Minor scale.

Example 4c

The next part of interest is an eight-bar section of the song that uses a pedal tone riff. It begins by playing notes on the seventh and sixth strings, then introduces a string skip to play the theme using wider intervals, before we shift the whole idea across to the sixth and fifth strings.

The melody of bars 1-2 is carried through to bars 3-4, played in a different position, but now the bass note accompaniment has changed.

In bar eight, we bring the seventh string back to end this section and lead into the next one.

Example 4d

The final section begins with a pedal tone idea, with the melody notes ascending the Bb Minor scale in bars 1-4. For bars 5-8, on the album recording I initially played full chords, but our producer suggested separating out the bass notes from the two-note chords sitting on top of them for sonic clarity in the mix, and now I tend to play it that way all the time. The part ends with some heavy chords and a final Bm triad octave that allows the low Bb to sustain.

Example 4e

♩ = 145

```
Bar 1                                          Bar 2
B|------------------------------------|--12-0--0--14-0--0--15-0--0--17-0--0--15-0--14-0--
  12-0--0--14-0--0--15-0--0--17-0--0--15-0--14-0--

Bar 3                                          Bar 4
  12-0--0--14-0--0--16-0--0--17-0--0--16-0--14-0--|--12--12--12--14--14--14--16--
                                                   |                          2--

Bar 5                      Bar 6                      Bar 7
  3-3-3-3-3-3-3-3-3-3-3-3-3-3-3-3--7-7-7-7-7-7-7-7-2-2-2-2-2-2-2-2--3-3-3-3-3-3-3-3-3-3-3-3-3-3-3-3--

Bar 8                      Bar 9    Bar 10        Bar 11
  7-7-7-7-7-7-7-7-2-2-2-2-2-2-2-2--2-----4-----8--------2--
                                    2-----4-----6--------2--
                                    0--------------------0--
```

7-string is also great for producing powerful low chordal ideas. *Into the Mouth of Hell We March* is a song from our fourth record *Shogun* that utilizes that powerful low punch, combining it with low pedal tone melodic sequences to construct the riff.

This first example is what is played during the introduction. Bars 1-2 use the seventh string for the root notes of the chords, and when we switch over to sixth string root notes, I will typically hook my thumb over the top of the neck. This just mutes the seventh string sufficiently for me to hit the chords with the same force as in the first two bars, and not be concerned about making unwanted string noise.

I actually wrote this idea sitting on a park bench in Copenhagen, playing on a Petrucci 7-string. It was a beautiful day and I decided to write something that sounded ominous and very Metal!

In terms of the chords used here, we begin with a B major power chord that includes the octave. We have the B bass note, the B octave stacked on top, then the 5th (F#) on top of that. For some reason, I decided to play this chord using an insane stretch (first finger on the seventh string, 1st fret; third finger on the fifth string, 3rd fret; fourth finger on the fourth string, 5th fret) using an *open voicing* (a chord that includes a string skip) rather than a *closed voicing* (notes arranged on adjacent strings).

In bar two we lower the top note of this chord shape by a half step, so we now have B, B octave, and F to form a tense sounding BMaj#11 (a.k.a. B major with a flattened 5th).

In bar three, the chord is an Ebsus2, constructed from the root (Eb), 5th (Bb) and suspended 2nd (F). In bar four, we lower the F note a whole step (Eb) and it becomes the octave in an Eb5 chord.

Example 4f

♩ = 145

The next example shows the rhythm guitar part used in the verse. For bars 1-2, this is based on the same chord structure as the previous example, but now we're picking out individual notes. The challenge here is to play the riff at album tempo at the same time as cleanly negotiating the wide string skips. My advice is to hold down the chord shape throughout, just as you did in the previous example.

I didn't set out to write a part that was difficult to play, by the way, it just naturally came out that way! As well as helping to sharpen your picking accuracy, it's a good riff to play to building your picking hand stamina.

Example 4g

The next example shows the chorus pattern to the song. It continues with the rhythm established in bars 3-4 of the previous example. Again, it calls for good picking hand stamina. You'll also need to ensure that your palm muting is on point, as all the chords are arranged on the bottom two strings, and you want to ensure that there is no noise being generated by the un-played strings.

Example 4h

The last 7-string song we'll look at is *What the Dead Men Say* from the record of the same name. You'll quickly see that this riff is all about the articulation that is used to bring it to life.

First, when we hit the A#/Bb note at the end of the first phrase in bar three, we'll apply some fast and very wide vibrato, which is essential for adding some emotive soulfulness into the line. Do this every time that four-note phrase is played.

For the rest of the riff, it's all about controlling the phrasing and the silence between phrases with careful palm muting to create its "push and pull" feel. You'll notice that the phrasing of the seventh string notes crosses the bar line. In fact, over the whole ten-bar section, there is an unsettled, ominous shifting feeling to the phrasing.

In bar eight, I rake across the strings with the pick perpendicular to the strings (i.e., sitting up with the pointed edge sitting on the strings, not tilted at an angle). I also tend to lightly rest my open fretting hand across all the strings and brush down the neck from high up to the nut.

Example 4i

Finally, a fun riff to learn and play from later in this song. Although it only uses the seventh string sparingly, it's useful to work your way through this one as there are plenty of twists and turns and it's a good workout for both fretting and picking hands.

When playing this riff, I keep my fretting hand first finger hovering around 7th position, just momentarily moving it down a half step to play the hammer-on from the 6th to 9th fret on the fifth string.

Have fun with this!

Example 4j

Chapter Five – Performance Piece: The Origin of Kiichi

To round off our journey, I wanted to close out the book with an original tune I wrote for 7-string guitar that was composed especially for this book. We'll break down all the parts of this instrumental tune and look at how the song is constructed, and how the different layers add to the overall finished piece.

But before we get into it, I wanted to pass on some general advice on songwriting/composition. I'd love for you to go away and write your own original tune after studying this chapter and share it on social media.

First, in Trivium, we've always set out to compose and play the kind of music we wanted to hear ourselves. I think that should be the first rule for any guitar player who wants to write authentic music that expresses who they are and what they're about. When you begin writing what you think other people want to hear, you're already compromised on two levels:

First, you've compromised your artistic integrity – you're not saying exactly what you want to say with your music.

Second, how can you second guess what others want to hear, and what will connect with them emotionally? That leads to making artistic compromises based on a vague idea you have of what others want to hear. My advice is to keep true to yourself and allow your music to emerge naturally, without setting any boundaries.

Next, get good at your craft. We can all improve our craft by learning more, getting more into music theory, learning about the art of songwriting from others, studying the musical structures of the tunes we love, etc., but the best way to get good at writing songs is by *writing songs*. So make a practice of composition, just as you'd set aside time to practice scales or riffs.

When I write, I try to avoid writing to a fixed or scheduled writing time. There's nothing worse than sitting down and saying to yourself, "OK, now I have to be creative for the next two hours!" When we impose that kind of pressure on ourselves, often inspiration is hard to come by.

I remember receiving a 1959 Les Paul Standard Reissue VOS from Gibson one time, which they sent me just to try out. It was easily the best Gibson I had ever played and, as a result, I just sat and played for fun and the inspiration flowed. Out of that zero pressure situation came riffs that featured on the album *In The Court of the Dragon*. Of course it's fine to be purposeful and workmanlike with your composition process, and great music can come out of that – but sometimes the best ideas just fall into our laps in moments like the one I've just described and we feel like we've captured lightning in a bottle.

Finally, remember that the more you play, the more likely you are to generate creative ideas that can turn into songs or instrumental pieces. The more you work on your craft as a musician, and the more you explore new ideas and listen to a wide range of music, the more lightning in a bottle moments you'll experience.

The Origin of Kiichi – Track Breakdown

Before getting into the examples, first familiarize yourself with the song by listening through it a couple of times. When you've done that, we can move on to look at the tune in sections and hear what the layered guitar parts are doing.

Example 5a shows the main riff of the tune. On the recording this is played in unison by two guitars, panned left and right to create a full, powerful sound.

Remember that while the chords indicated and positions on the neck relate to B Minor, the recorded pitch will sound a half step lower, as the guitar is detuned and the low B string is now Bb. It would be more confusing to call the chord Bbm when we're playing at the 7th fret!

With this riff, we're using the open seventh string as a root note pedal tone in bars 1-4 and 9-12 where the chord is Bm, then moving the root on the 7th string accordingly to spell out the other chord changes. The melody notes come from the B Natural Minor scale, which has the notes: B, C#, D, E, F#, G, A.

Notice that the melody stays the same when the chord changes in bars 5-6, but is modified slightly over the A chord in bar seven. The final note in bar seven is a Bb. Over the A major chord, this note is the b9 and it creates a moment of tension as it clashes with the root note of the chord.

In fact, what's going on here is that the Bb is a chord tone of the F#7 (enharmonically an A#) that falls in bar eight, and we're anticipating that change by playing the 3rd of the chord a beat early. This is a compositional device used in music ranging from classical to jazz as a way of creating a tension (by playing "wrong notes" if you like) that is quickly resolved.

Example 5a

In the next 16-bar section of the tune, the first guitar continues to play the main riff, while the second guitar plays a harmony part pitched a 3rd interval above the original.

When I'm composing an instrumental tune like this, I like to focus on layering up parts to create new sections. We can build multiple different parts this way, then choose which ones we want to repeat or adapt later on. Play this along to the previous example.

Example 5b

Since the riff section had been building for a while, I felt it was time for a breakdown section in the song at this point. During this section, the guitars continue to play in harmony, but the overall feel is darker than the uplifting energy of the riff section. First, here is the lower guitar part for you to learn.

This breakdown is mostly rhythm oriented, but it's punctuated with embellishment licks, which are a nice feature to play in harmony. This section is also unusual as it has an odd number of bars (eleven).

Example 5c

Next, here is the harmony guitar part for the breakdown section. Notice that the second guitar drops out of harmony and into unison for bars 10-11. This small detail, the fact that the breakdown has an odd number of bars, and because the chord progression ascends here, all help this section feel like the gateway to something new in the tune.

Example 5d

73

It's in bars 10-11 that the lead guitar is heard for the first time. It plays the following line over the two-bar tag that leads us into the next section of the tune.

Here we're using a big-picture take on the idea of *contrary motion.* This is a compositional device, often used in classical music and other genres, where two lines move in opposite directions i.e., one line ascends while the other descends.

I say it's a "big-picture" take, because instead of two melodic lines moving in contrary motion, here we have some big powerful chords ascending, while the lead guitar melody descends. The result is a more complex harmonic structure.

Example 5e

After a breakdown section like this, it would be tempting to just return to the main theme of the tune and repeat it, but why not build on the previous idea and take a fresh direction instead to keep the listener engaged?

Since we've now introduced the lead guitar as a third voice in the composition, here we use it to play a melodic theme and create a new section of the tune. The chords change here too, and this section functions as a kind of bridge. This part comprises four separate guitar parts, which we'll look at it turn.

Guitar one plays this low, straightforward riff, sonically holding down the bottom end and providing a foundation for the other parts to work off.

Example 5f

G ... Bm A/C# D A

```
T
A
B  --3-3-3-3-3-3-3-3--|--3-3-3-3-3-3-3-3--|--0-0-0-0-2-2-2-2--|--3-3-3-3--5-5-5-5--:
```

Guitar two plays in unison to create a full, powerful sound. As a small detail, the part is identical other than the final four notes of bar four, where a harmony note is played. This might seem inconsequential but when the other parts are layered on top, it enhances the overall sonic picture.

Example 5g

G ... Bm

```
T
A
B  --3-3-3-3-3-3-3-3--|--3-3-3-3-3-3-3-3--|--0-0-0-0-0-0-0-0--|--0-0-0-0--5-5-5-5--
```

G ... Bm A/C# D A

```
T
A
B  --3-3-3-3-3-3-3-3--|--3-3-3-3-3-3-3-3--|--0-0-0-0-2-2-2-2--|--3-3-3-3--5-5-5-5--
```

The next two layers of this section feature lead guitar parts. Here is the first. It's a simple but strong melodic motif, broken up with a one-bar embellishment at the end of each eight bar section.

Example 5h

The second lead guitar part plays the same line an octave lower to support the lead guitar and thicken out the sound. Harmony guitar parts always sound great and create interest in a composition. They can be impressive to listen to, especially if the line they are playing has some complexity to it. However, if you're looking for raw power and energy, playing in unison in different octaves is a great choice that can produce spine-tingling effects.

Example 5i

The next eight-bar section of the tune introduces another breakdown, which will serve as the launching point for the next main section of the song. It's comprised of three layered guitar parts and all eight bars are based on a single note.

The use of just one note adds to the sense of anticipation in the composition – like something is about to be revealed. This is another compositional tool you can consider using when writing your own songs: it's like a pedal tone, but the whole band plays it for tension and release.

The first of the three parts just plays the open seventh string, first as sustained notes, then as a syncopated low pulse.

Example 5j

On top of this, the second guitar plays a pedal tone riff that bounces off the open seventh string. In bars 1-4, the previous guitar part is just providing a low drone to this new, syncopated riff. But then in bars 5-8 they begin to react to one another, and the previous part moves into a syncopated rhythm that fits around this new riff.

Use the audio examples to play both these parts, one over the other, to see the effect they create.

Example 5k

Finally, this section features a lead line that sits on top. First, a single note is played and sustained, which adds some texture and contrast to the low parts. Then, in bars 5-6 we play a slow "outside to inside" bend. The idea here is to play two notes on adjacent strings a half step apart, creating a deliberately dissonant sound. One of these notes will be in key and one will not.

Leaving the "in key" note ringing, we bend the dissonant note slowly up a half step until it reaches the same pitch as the "in" note and we hear a pleasing unison sound. This is another useful method for creating tension and release.

Example 51

For the next sixteen bars, both rhythm guitars play this syncopated bassline in unison. Take a moment to master the rhythm here and play it cleanly with good palm muting.

The best way to go about this is to slow it right down and count it in 1/16th notes while you lock the rhythm into muscle memory. Here is the pattern for bar one, with the played notes highlighted in bold:

1-e-**&**-a, **2**-e-**&**-a, **3**-e-**&**-a, **4**-e-**&**-a

Note that in the first group of four notes, we play two 1/16th notes (on the "1" and the "e") followed by two 1/8th notes. The first 1/8th note falls on the "&" of beat 1, while the second falls directly on beat 2.

This pattern of playing two 1/16th notes followed by two 1/8th notes is repeated in each group of four notes – we just displace them by playing the second group starting on the "&" of beat 3, making them cross the bar line.

The rhythm changes on every fourth bar as you can see in the TAB. Here, the rhythm is simpler. Counted in 1/16th notes it is:

1-e-**&**-a, **2**-e-**&**-a, **3**-e-**&**-a, **4**-e-**&**-a

Practice this a few times until you've got it down. Also take the idea away and play around with it – it's a good drill for testing out syncopated rhythms, creating interest by playing a simple phrase and moving it to different beats of the bar.

Example 5m

The two lead guitars play a pedal tone harmony sequence over the syncopated groove. Here is the lower part, which dovetails together with the low bass notes.

Example 5n

Now, here is the higher harmony. The harmony notes are arranged a 3rd above the previous part but notice that both guitars play the bass notes in unison. This enables us to create some interest with the harmony, but add some real punch to the bass part, with all the layered parts hitting those low notes.

Example 50

During the next eight-bar section of the tune, the low rhythm parts begin to play a root and 5th power chord unison part, using the open seventh string. The syncopation of the rhythm changes here. Here it is counted in 1/16th notes:

1-**e**-**&**-a, **2**-**e**-**&**-a, **3**-e-**&**-**a**, **4**-e-**&**-**a**

As I alluded to a moment ago, you can take a very simple idea (a single note played four times) and create numerous rhythmic ideas from it by varying the lengths of the notes and displacing them to different beats in the bar.

Here, in the first group of four notes we're playing two 1/16th notes followed by an 1/8th note, but then adding a 1/4 note. In the second group of four notes, we go back to our original pattern of two 1/16th notes and two 1/8th notes. The result is that the rhythm is broken up in a new way.

During this section, the first lead guitar plays the exact same pattern used in bars 1-8 of Example 5n, while the second lead guitar plays the same pattern used in bars 1-8 of Example 5o.

Example 5p

Now we move into the new section of the tune we've been building up to. If we've done our job well of gradually increasing the tension coming into this part, then we should now reach a real crescendo as the guitar solo begins.

The solo lasts for sixteen bars. Before we look at it, let's look at the underlying chord sequence that supports the solo.

The whole idea of this sequence is one of a constantly building crescendo, so rather than playing a simple accompanying rhythm and letting this section be carried by the guitar solo, the rhythm part also builds via ascending chord voicings.

Bar one begins with a Bm root plus 5th power chord. Then we move through a series of chords in the key, playing a couple of them as inversions (with a note other than the root of the chord in the bass), so that the bassline ascends. The A/C# chord in bar one, for example, is a straight A major chord voiced with the 3rd (C#) in the bass and the root note on top. The D/F# in bar two uses the same idea.

This idea continues in bars 9-16 when the root notes of the chords are moved across onto the sixth string, so that the bassline can ascend higher.

Example 5q

Now let's break down the guitar solo and look at some of the ideas being used. We'll split it into three parts, beginning with the first eight bars. There are several approaches we can take when constructing a solo. If the chord changes are sparse or slower, we might think more about the chords being used and target certain chord tones during our improvisation, so that we effectively spell out the harmony for the listener. Alternatively, we might decide to just blow over the changes, allowing our melodic lines and licks to flow over the chords without targeting specific notes.

At this point in the song, the backing chords are a constantly moving landscape because we've chosen to build the energy with those ascending chord voicings, so the lead guitar is free to add its distinct voice by flowing freely across the changes.

We begin the solo with what blues players call a "question and answer" or "call and response" phrase. The call phrase is posed in bars 1-2 and the response is played in bars 3-4. Although it uses different notes, the phrasing is identical. The idea is that it sounds like a conversation, and it's this vocal phrasing that is such an important element of the blues.

In bars 6-8 I play a fast ascending line. All the notes here come from the B Natural Minor scale (B, C#, D, E, F#, G, A).

At the beginning of bar six, you can play the starting B note either on the 7th fret of the sixth string, then slide up into 9th position for the rest of the phrase, or start with your fretting hand in 9th position and lead off the lick by playing the 12th fret of the seventh string with your pinkie finger, as shown below.

I prefer the latter to minimize the movement the fretting hand needs to make, but go with whatever is more comfortable for you. It depends somewhat on the strength of your pinkie!

The line is composed mostly of 1/16th notes but at the end of bar seven into bar eight, I speed up, moving into 1/16th note triplet phrasing. It's difficult to represent this kind of idea clearly and precisely in notation, so I recommend the following method for learning it (and any other challenging line):

- Listen carefully to the audio to get the shape of the line in your ears

- Play through the line slowly, out of tempo, to get your fingers used to the movements

- Play the line slowly to a metronome and work on the phrasing

- Gradually increase the metronome and bring the line up to performance speed

Example 5r

I consider myself the least shreddy guitar player in Trivium – that's Corey's domain – so I like to use melodic motifs and sequences in my solos. The next four bars use a sequenced lick arranged on the top three strings.

After the sustained bend in bar one, we lead into the sequenced lick with a three-note phrase. In bars 1-2 the note choices come from the B Natural Minor scale. In bars 3-4, to create a little more tension, we switch to the B Phrygian scale (B, C, D, E, F#, G, A)

B Phrygian has only one note different to B Natural Minor – a C instead of a C# – but that note makes a big difference. It gives us the very tense and dark sounding b2 interval that is so much a part of the modern Metal sound. In the first phrase of bar three, we hit that b2 interval while playing over an Em chord, which implies a harmony of Emb6.

The sequence itself doesn't follow a regular pattern, so learning it is a case of slowly working through the pattern and rhythms and training them into muscle memory.

Example 5s

The final four bars of the solo feature a fast, descending sequenced lick, mostly played in 1/16th notes, but slowing to 1/8th notes in the final bar, where the line ascends and holds a final note to finish.

In terms of the chord progression, this is the part of the solo where we transfer the root notes of the chords onto the sixth string so that we can keep ascending. This means that the tonal center here is more E minor than B minor to begin with, though we remain in the same key. It therefore made sense here to switch to the E Phrygian scale (E, F, G, A, B, C, D) for bars 1-2. Then we drop back into the B Natural Minor scale for bar three.

Look out for the rhythm at the beginning of bar one. Although this line is played as nearly all 1/16th notes, it leads in with a faster 1/16th note triplet phrase. I will always play a line like this with strict alternate down-up picking. Work out your fretting hand movements slowly to begin with, to achieve the most comfortable fingering that suits you, before bringing it up to speed.

Example 5t

Following on from the guitar solo there is a 16-bar section that is a repeat of one we played earlier. The guitar parts laid out in examples 5f, 5g and 5h are played here, repeating the main motif of the song. Then, without warning, there is a key change that shifts everything up a whole step. The low guitars play this bassline in unison.

Example 5u

A very useful compositional tool we can use when songwriting is to reference a motif or a longer melodic theme, but make changes to it – either in the harmony or in the way the motif is played. There are a number of different takes on this core idea.

You're almost bound to have a heard a melodic motif played in a movie soundtrack, one time over a major chord sequence, then the same idea played over a minor chord sequence. The result is that the motif can sound happy or melancholy or sinister by making changes to the harmony – all while keeping the motif the same.

Another approach is to keep your original chord progression and move the melodic motif to begin on a different note or start on a different beat of the bar. This way, you keep the motif note-for-note, but now it has a different effect because the notes fall on different chords.

Finally, you can alter the tonality of the motif itself by transposing it to a different key, so that the listener can still hang onto the motif, but hear it expressed in a new way. I opted for this latter approach and, rather than changing to a relative key, just shifted up a whole step to create an element of surprise and give the tune a further lift.

The next two examples show the motif transposed to the new key. First, the higher part:

Example 5v

Lead guitar two plays the same line an octave lower.

Example 5w

Now we come to the final sixteen bars of the tune. To end on a high, in this section the low rhythm guitars play a harmony riff while the two lead guitars play a fast harmony lick on the top three strings. Here is rhythm guitar one's part. The effect I was going for here was to play something like a classical, almost Bach-like etude.

Example 5x

Bm

G **A** **F#7**

Rhythm guitar two plays this complementary part, doubling up bass notes but harmonizing with the high notes.

Example 5y

Finally, let's look at what the higher harmony guitars are playing during this section. Below is lead guitar one's part. For a sequenced lick such as this, you can either use economy picking or alternate picking.

My preference is to alternate pick most things, if possible, but if you're an economy picker, this lick is arranged nicely for that technique too, so go with what you're most comfortable with. There's no doubt that it's challenging to alternate pick this at full tempo.

The line opens with a Bm arpeggio inversion (F#, D, B, F#) that is repeated over bars 1-2. In bars 3-4, the underlying chord is still Bm, but the arpeggio notes change to G, D, B, F# in order – an inversion of a GMaj7 arpeggio.

The idea of superimposing one arpeggio over another is one that is commonly used in jazz-fusion music and is a core idea in the playing of guitarists like Greg Howe. It works because GMaj7 is chord VI in the key of B Minor, and when played over a Bm chord its intervals produce a different sonic effect, without any clashing notes.

In bars 5-6, we're playing a simple G major arpeggio over the G chord, and in bar seven an A major arpeggio.

When we get to bar eight, the underlying harmony is an F#7 chord. Over this we're playing a G diminished arpeggio. This is another technique borrowed from jazz-fusion. To create more interesting tensions over a dominant 7 chord, you can play a diminished arpeggio whose root note is a half step above, i.e., Gdim over F#7.

Example 5z

To complete the picture, the second lead guitar plays the high harmony that mirrors the previous part a 3rd above.

Example 5z1

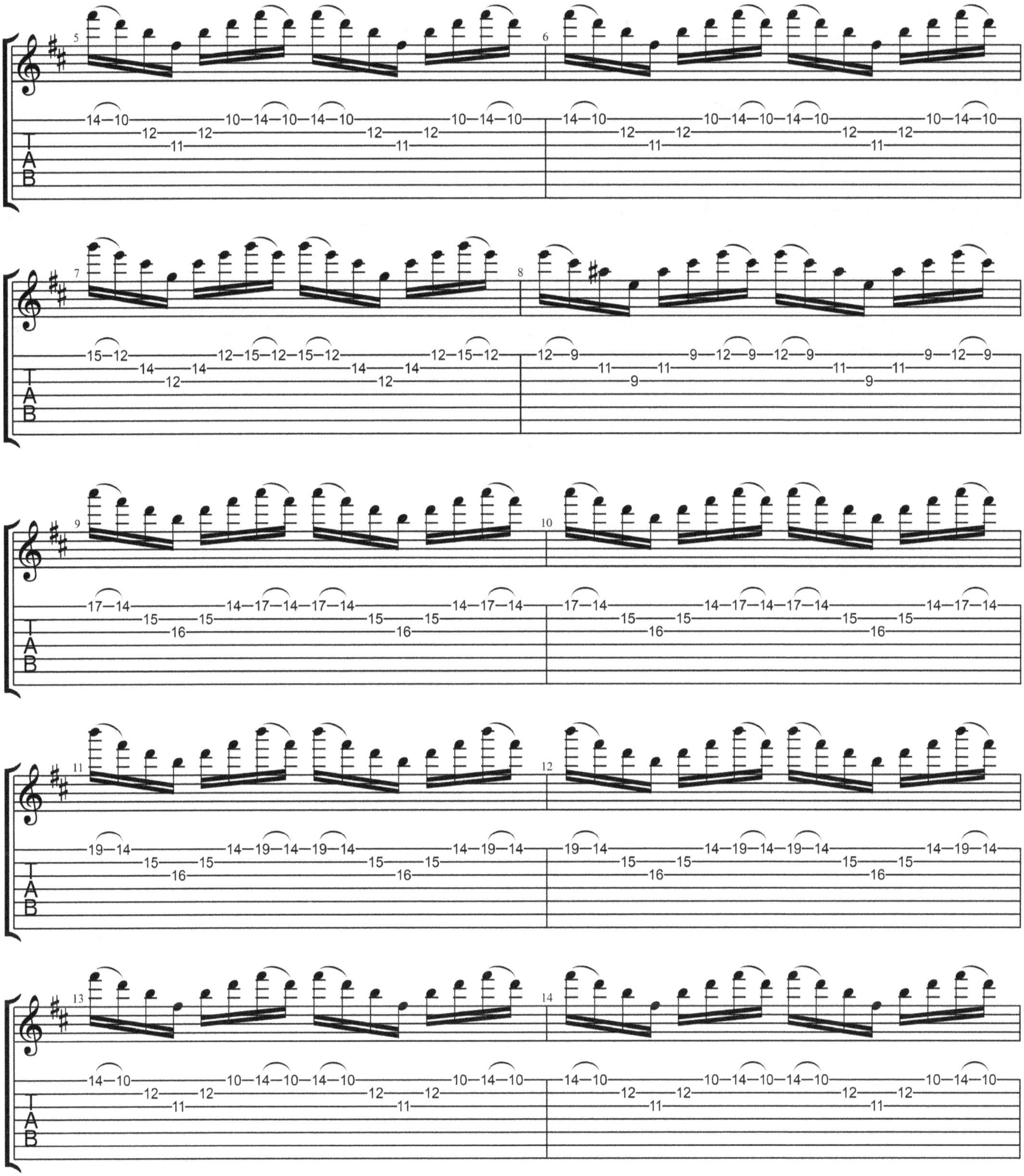

We've worked through all the sections of this tune, breaking down and analyzing each guitar part. Have fun playing all the different lines and feel free to take and adapt the riffs to invent your own ideas. You can also have a go at composing your own solo over the backing track in the audio download.

Connect with Matt Heafy

You can keep up with what I'm doing and connect with me on these social channels:

https://instagram.com/matthewkheafy

https://x.com/matthewkheafy

https://twitch.com/matthewkheafy

https://youtube.com/matthewkheafy

https://facebook.com/matthewkheafy

https://discord.gg/matthewkheafy

www.ingramcontent.com/pod-product-compliance
Lightning Source LLC
Chambersburg PA
CBHW081434090426
42740CB00017B/3303